Sabine Baring-Gould

The Death and Resurrection of Jesus

Ten Lectures for Holy Week and Easter

Sabine Baring-Gould

The Death and Resurrection of Jesus
Ten Lectures for Holy Week and Easter

ISBN/EAN: 9783743384064

Manufactured in Europe, USA, Canada, Australia, Japa

Cover: Foto ©Lupo / pixelio.de

Manufactured and distributed by brebook publishing software (www.brebook.com)

Sabine Baring-Gould

The Death and Resurrection of Jesus

The Death and Resurrection of Jesus.

TEN LECTURES FOR HOLY WEEK AND EASTER.

BY

S. BARING GOULD, M.A.,

AUTHOR OF "THE BIRTH OF JESUS." "NAZARETH AND CAPERNAUM." "THE PASSION OF JESUS." "THE TRIALS OF JESUS." "THE SEVEN LAST WORDS." "THE WAY OF SORROWS." ETC.

New York:
JAMES POTT & CO., 14 & 16, ASTOR PLACE.
1888.

Preface.

These Ten Lectures continue the Commentary on the Passion and Resurrection of Christ, contained in my volumes

    I. The Passion of Jesus.
    II. The Trials of Jesus.
    III. The Way of Sorrows.
    IV. The Seven Last Words.

This forms the fifth of the series. Should the publishers feel justified in continuing it, the sixth will complete this series with the record from the Appearance of Christ to the Ten on Easter Day in the Evening to the Descent of the Holy Ghost at Pentecost. I began another series, of which the first was "The Birth of Jesus," and the next "Nazareth and Capernaum," with the intention of their forming a Commentary on the Life of our Lord to the Passion, but there has been comparatively little demand for these volumes, so this series will not be continued.

Lew Trenchard, N. Devon,
    Nov. 21, 1887.

Contents.

I.
The Risen Saints.
(Suitable for All Saints.)
S. MATT. XXVII. 52, 53.

"The graves were opened; and many bodies of the Saints which slept arose, and came out of the graves after His Resurrection, and went into the holy city, and appeared unto many." — 1

II.
The Rent Veil.
S. MATT. XXVII. 51.

"Behold, the vail of the Temple was rent in twain from the top to the bottom." — 11

III.
The Pierced Side.
S. JOHN XIX. 34.

"One of the soldiers with a spear pierced His side, and forthwith came thereout blood and water." — 19

IV.
The Descent from the Cross.
S. MATT. XXVII. 57, 58.

"When the even was come, there came a rich man of Arimathea, named Joseph, who also himself was Jesus' disciple: he went to Pilate, and begged the body of Jesus." — 27 viii.

V.
The Entombment.
S. LUKE XXIII. 53.
"He laid it in a sepulchre that was hewn in stone, wherein never man before was laid." ... 34

VI.
The Great Sabbath.
S. LUKE XXIII. 56.
"They returned . . . and rested the Sabbath Day, according to the Commandment." ... 42

VII.
The Spirits in Prison.
1 PETER III. 19.
"He went and preached unto the spirits in prison." ... 50

VIII.
The Resurrection.
S. MATT. XXVIII. 2-4.
"Behold, there was a great earthquake: for the angel of the Lord descended from Heaven, and came and rolled back the stone from the door, and sat upon it. His countenance was like lightning, and his raiment white as snow; and for fear of him the keepers did shake, and became as dead men." ... 58

IX.
The Appearance to Mary Magdalene.
S. JOHN XX. 11.
"And Mary stood without the sepulchre, weeping." ... 67

X.
The Way to Emmaus.
S. MARK XVI. 12.
"After that He appeared in another form unto two of them, as they walked, and went into the country." ... 75

Appendix. On the site of the Holy Sepulchre.

The Death and Resurrection of Jesus.

I.

The Risen Saints.

S. MATT. XXVII. 52, 53.

"The graves were opened; and many bodies of the Saints which slept arose, and came out of the graves after His Resurrection, and went into the holy city, and appeared unto many."

THE sun declined on that Good Friday when Christ hung on the Cross. With a loud cry He gave up the ghost, as the priests standing before the gates of Nicanor, that led into the Temple, blew a loud trumpet-blast to announce that the Paschal Feast was beginning.

And as, at the Last Day, at the setting of the sun on the earth for the last time, the trumpet of the Archangel will sound, and the graves will be opened, and the dead arise, so was it now at the last day of the Old Covenant, at the close of the first period of the World's History.

Good Friday was the day on which the hinge of History turned; it was the last day of the Old History, and in several ways on it was the final judgment scene rehearsed. Then the sun will be darkened, and the moon turnèd into blood, and now there is darkness over all the earth. Then the sign of the Son of Man will appear in Heaven, and now it stands against the sky, bearing on it the body of the Son of Man. Then the veil of the Heavens will be rent asunder and rolled up, and now the symbolical veil of the Temple is torn from the top to the bottom. Then there will be earthquakes, and now the rocks are rent; then will be the opening of all graves, and now the tombs give up their dead.

The incident of the rising Saints is given only by S. Matthew, and it is an incident not often commented upon, and when commented on is treated as a difficult one, hard to be explained. It is an incident that deserves more notice than is usually accorded to it, for it is one of those few incidents recorded in Scripture which show us something of the relation in which the world of spirits stands to the world of the living.

It was customary among the Romans for the great families, the patricians, who had the *jus imaginum*, at a funeral to have a train of masqueraders attend, who wore wax masks resembling the faces of the ancestors of the deceased, masks taken from the gallery of ancestral portrait-busts and statues. The meaning of this curious rite was this. The mourners were taken to represent the dead of the patrician's family, who rose and came forth from the world of spirits to salute and welcome and attend their descendant at his decease. It was the same at the funeral of an emperor, only then there appeared men dressed in imperial purple, and crowned, and with masks to resemble the former emperors and great men of old Rome, come forth from the shadow realm to welcome the dead entering into their nether world.*

But, indeed, the idea that the dead appeared when death approaches is a very common one, and there is hardly a nation in which such stories are not found of ancestral spirits which appear as a death token. And, I may add, it is in the experience of many who have had to do with death-beds that the dying do either see, or believe they see, relatives long dead, appear to them before their eyes finally close, as though they had come to meet them on their way, and accompany them to the far off land.

I do not mean to assert as a certain fact that such apparitions *do* take place, but there can be no question whatever that the dying do very often believe they see their lost relatives, and the dying face suddenly brightens, a smile breaks out on the lips, and the hands are stretched out with an exclamation of recognition, and a name, or names, uttered of one or more long dead and almost forgotten.

Now this phenomenon, which is incontestible, this belief which is very widely spread, bears some relation to the fact

* Polybius vi. 53; Pliny xxxv. 2.

of the apparitions on our Lord's decease, and I may almost say that this incident in the Gospel record gives strength to the belief that a much closer relation subsists between the seen and unseen worlds than is generally allowed. As our Lord gave up the ghost, the graves were opened, and the ancient patriarchs appeared.

At the central point of the World's History, the Lord of both worlds, after having wrought out the salvation of men, descends into the realm of spirits. According to the genealogy given by S. Luke, there were seventy-seven generations of men to Christ; seventy-seven generations which had sinned against God. And now He, Who, by taking our human nature on Him, has become our brother, brings forgiveness to the seventy-seven generations, prisoners of hope, waiting till, by the blood of the Covenant, they should obtain release.

We know how the dead in faith looked forward to this day with longing. "Your father Abraham," said Christ, "rejoiced to see My day; he saw it, and was glad" (S. John viii. 6); and on Tabor, Moses and Elias appeared speaking with Him concerning "His decease, which He should accomplish in Jerusalem." (S. Luke ix. 31.) Indeed, aged Simeon may be taken as the spokesman of all the faithful, living and dead, when he uttered his song of praise on receiving the Child Jesus in his arms in the Temple.

We are not told that the bodies of the Saints rose till after the Resurrection, when Christ being raised became the first fruits of them that slept, but the graves were opened at His death, and the spirits, doubtless, were then seen by Christ's closing eyes, gathered on Calvary to receive Him, and when He rose they attended Him from the place of Hades again, this time clothed in their restored bodies.

Before the Reformation the Doctrine of the Communion of Saints had been strained to sanction practices which were inconsistent with pure Christianity. The Saints were thrust into undue prominence to the obscuration of Christ; but we have suffered ever since the Reformation from the reaction, and have come to give no thought at all to the dead in Christ, and to treat the article of the Communion of Saints as if it had no meaning, was of no practical importance, and did not find a place in the Apostles' Creed. Yet this article would not be there unless it were of vital importance, and we may well ask ourselves whether the neglect of this article is not a serious sin of defect in our religion, just as the exaggeration of this doctrine was a sin of excess and superstition. In our Creed we profess our belief in one Holy Catholic Church, the Communion of Saints; it is an article which is double, and yet one. There is but one Catholic Church, as there is but one Lord, one faith, one baptism, but in this one Church there are two parts, the Church of the living and the Church of the dead; as surely as we who are baptized and keep the faith belong to the Catholic Church, so surely do those who have kept the faith and have entered into their rest belong to the Catholic Church. As we are brethren one of another, who are alive, so do they who are gone belong to us, and we to them; we are all one body in Christ. And as we who are alive have duties to discharge to one another, and responsibilities one to another, so is it with the dead in Christ, they have their offices of love and brotherhood to discharge towards us, and we in like manner towards them.

In the Cathedral of Strassburg all the clerestory windows are filled with figures of Saints and Angels in glory. The lower aisle windows represent the acts and miracles of our Lord and the World's History. Beneath the floor lie the dead, and the idea contained in this arrangement is the unity of the Church. Aloft are the glorified hierarchy of Angels and Saints and just men made perfect, in the midst are we, the living, and beneath are those who rest, and have not attained unto the fulness of perfection. Above the Church triumphant, in the midst the Church militant, beneath the Church expectant.

The whole of the Christian life is one of growth, and we have no reason whatever to suppose that we come to a standstill in the spiritual life at death, but rather that we pass from one stage of development to another. We have a thousand analogies in nature, and we may well expect that eternity will be a succession of ages of infinite progress, of growth into the likeness of Christ, of deepening of the love of God, of increase of spiritual discernment, of widening of knowledge.

Can we suppose that when those who have loved us on earth pass into the unseen world they have ceased to interest themselves in us? S. Paul teaches us the contrary, when he speaks of us as running in a race with multitudes looking on, no longer now in the arena, but on the several ranges of Heaven, some higher, some lower, all with eyes fixed on us, all eager for our success, and uttering their acclamations of encouragement.

Is it conceivable that the mother who dies has not a word of prayer for her child on earth, battling its orphaned way through temptations? Is it not probable that every human affection is by death purified of all selfishness, but does not cease, nay rather, is intensified and spiritualized. And if spiritualized and intensified, must it not break forth into prayer? Is it not simply inconceivable, is it not only conceivable as a contradiction to the whole tenor of Christianity, that human love should live on and be denied expression? Would it not be intense agony to one who has passed into the presence of God to be refused permission there to continue that intercession for the dear ones on earth which was allowed and even commanded to be made when in the body?

And, again, have we no duties to perform towards the dead in Christ? Is that article in the Creed one—the only one that is void of practical force, which is not to be turned into a source of action?

If the condition of the spiritual life be one of progress, of infinite progress, then we may help by our prayers those who have passed into the second stage of development, that their sins may be forgiven, and that their growth in light and perfection may be continued.

Is there, we ask, some efficacious means of entering into close communion with the dead in Christ? To this question we can answer with the unanimous voice of early Christianity—that in the Holy Communion that bond is drawn in the closest and tenderest manner. When S. Ignatius was martyred, about A.D. 108, the eye witnesses of his death wrote in their circular letter to the Church, "We note the day and hour (of his death) that we may assemble at the time of his martyrdom, and give token of our communion with this noble confessor and witness of Christ." That is to say, they assembled for the liturgy; and this we know was the universal custom of the early Church, the tombs of the martyrs being used as the altars at which the Eucharist was celebrated.

In the Vatican is perhaps the most glorious picture of all that Raphael ever painted, the so-called Disputa. It represents Christ enthroned in Heaven holding up His hands and shewing His wounds, with the Saints seated on His right and left, and the firmament thrilling with light, and angelic forms half seen among the rays of supernal light. Below is the living Church made up of kings and princes, bishops, doctors, warriors, holy men and women of every age and degree, on the steps leading to an altar; and on this altar, as the central point, the link binding Heaven and earth in one, is the Blessed Sacrament of the Eucharist.

That, indeed, which is the central act of Christian worship, the one great sun of the spiritual system of the Church, that is the bond between Heaven and earth, the link between the visible and the invisible, the means whereby we, being united to Christ, are united in and through Him with the Saints and faithful departed.

In many of the old heathen faiths it was held that there were times of the year, as the solstices and equinoxes, when at night the doors of the unseen world were thrown open, and the dead appeared and rushed with the wind, wailing over the face of the earth; and many a fable was told of how men out at night on such occasions had seen the spirits sweep by on the wings of the storm.

On All Saints and All Souls we may look up and see the dead, not as the heathen thought, in wild unrest, but waiting for the consummation of all things, one with us in the object of our worship, one with us in common subjection to the one King, one with us in the same great family, one in the same hope, the resurrection and restoration of all things, one in the same mysterious spiritual life, which is ever striving after perfection, and is in itself capable of infinite perfectibility.

II.

The Rent Veil.

S. MATT. XXVII. 51.

"Behold, the vail of the Temple was rent in twain from the top to the bottom."

THE work of redemption was accomplished; with the exceeding bitter cry, the soul of the Saviour left His body, and at the parting, the rending of soul from body, the veil in the Temple was sharply torn from top to bottom. From henceforth the way into the Holy of Holies is open to all. God is no more veiled in the Temple and rites of the Jews; He reveals Himself to all mankind.

Every year once, on the Great Day of Atonement, the High Priest was wont to pass behind the veil into the Holy of Holies, bearing the blood of the slain ram. And now the true Sacrifice has been offered, of which this was but a shadow and figure; and with the rent veil we are shewn that the time of figure and shadow is over, for the reality has come. Hitherto only one, the High Priest, might enter with the atoning blood, but now the way is open to all.

"Having, brethren, boldness," writes the author of the Epistle to the Hebrews, "to enter into the holiest by the

Blood of Jesus, by a new and living way, which He hath consecrated for us, that is to say, His flesh, and having an High Priest over the House of God, let us draw near with a true heart, in full assurance of faith."

The veil of the Temple which was rent was that which hung between the Holy of Holies and the Holy Place, and behind it was the Ark of the Covenant in the early Temple, but that old Ark was no longer in the Temple after the return from captivity.

In the Tabernacle there had been one veil, and so also in the Temple, before the destruction of Jerusalem, but when the Temple was rebuilt by Ezra after the pattern of that which had been destroyed, some difficulty arose as to the position of the veil—whether it hung within the golden pillars that sustained the roof, or without them, that is to say, whether the pillars were to be included in the Holy of Holies, or in the outer place. To get over this difficulty, a double veil, or rather two veils, were used, one outside the pillars towards what we may call the Nave, and one within, towards the Chancel.*

When in the Gospel we are told that the veil was rent, almost certainly both veils were torn, and fell apart, exposing the Holy of Holies, but in the Gospel only veil, in the singular, is used, because the double curtain was taken to

---

* Bab Ioma, fol. 51, 2. Maimon in Beth habbechira, c. iv.

represent the single veil ordered by God to divide the Holy of Holies from the outer Holy Place. The veil was of the utmost magnificence, woven of purple, and red, and blue, and white, and with the figures of the Cherubim on it, and starred with gold thread interwoven with the colours.

Outside the veil was the perpetual lamp that was on no account allowed to go out. We learn from Jewish sources that forty years before the destruction of Jerusalem, suddenly one day the lamp went out, and never again would burn regularly. When it was re-lighted so as to fill the Temple with light at night, it went out of itself before daybreak.

We are told of other signs that took place at the same time. The great stone threshold of the Temple was snapped asunder by the earthquake which rent the rocks, and opened the graves.* And the doors of the Temple swung open of their own accord.

Another token of Divine wrath is also recorded by the Jews as having taken place at the same time. They relate that on the Great Day of Atonement, when a scarlet cord, which was bound round the horns of the scapegoat, and which attached it to the Temple gates, it was wont, up to this time, to lose its blood-red colour, and turn white, when the High Priest laid on the goat's head the sins of the people. This was regarded as a pledge that the trans-

* In the Gospel of the Hebrews, as quoted by S. Jerome.

gressions of the House of Israel were remitted every year. But on this year, for the first time, the bloodstain remained and was not miraculously bleached. In vain did the High Priest recite over the goat the sins of the people, and plead with Jehovah for pardon; thenceforth the outer token that God heard the prayer and granted absolution ceased to be given. Wonderful does this seem to us—this recorded by the Jews themselves—and to remember how they had called down the blood of Christ on their own heads and on those of their children. Moreover, hitherto the lot had always fallen on the left-hand goat, but from this time on to the destruction of the Temple it fell on the goat on the right hand. *

In the Church of the Holy Sepulchre, in the chapel of Golgotha, is shown a rent in the limestone rock supposed to have been made by the earthquake that took place at the giving up of the ghost by Christ. The crack in the rock is now closed with a grating, and is choked up to about a foot; but we know from early accounts that formerly it was a deep cleft—so deep that popular fancy supposed it went down to the centre of the earth. Accumulations of rubbish have filled it since then, and now all that shews is the mouth of the fissure, apparently made by an earthquake. Such cracks in the rock are not infrequent,

* Ioma, fol. 39, 2; and fol. 43, 3.

on occasions of a convulsion of the earth. From Zechariah (xiv. 4) we hear of one occurring at Jerusalem, when the Mount of Olives was split; and Josephus records one which took place at Jerusalem, when half of the mountain on the east side of the valley of Kidron fell, and masses of the rock were hurled half-way up the side of the opposite slope. On this occasion the roads and the royal gardens were buried. In 1783 an earthquake in Calabria rent the earth, and formed a chasm at Oppido five hundred feet long, and to a depth of over 200 feet. Whether the split in the rock in the church over Golgotha be one made at the time of Christ's death or by the earthquake at the Resurrection, or on any other occasion, cannot be said for certain; but this is determined, that on the rocky height which tradition has unswervingly identified with Calvary the rock is rent asunder by seismic force, and that the chasm in the Middle Ages was so profound that it was supposed to go down to the centre of the world. In all probability, if the site be accepted as the true scene of Christ's death, then we may well suppose that when He died, uttering a loud cry, the rock on which the Cross was planted was cleft asunder; for the Centurion and those who stood by saw the wonder of the earthquake, and were themselves profoundly shaken by it in their consciences.

"Now when the Centurion, and they that were with

him, watching Jesus, saw the earthquake,¹ and those things that were done, they feared greatly, saying, Truly this was the Son of God." (S. Matt. xxvii. 54.)

Of the signs, only the darkness, and the earthquake, and the opening of the graves, were visible by those on Calvary. To the present day, in a chapel at the foot of the rock, are the remains of old Jewish graves cut in the rock. These would be closed with stone slabs revolving in grooves. When the earth shook, these slabs rolled back, or were split and fell outward. We must imagine the Centurion on his horse, the same who had led the escort to Calvary, and whose duty it was to remain to the end. He had heard the mocking cry of the Jews, "If Thou be the Son of God, come down from the Cross." He was a man with some feeling in him for the Victim, for he had arrested the procession to Calvary and relieved Christ of the burden of the Cross to lay it on the shoulders of Simon of Cyrene. He had been awed by the stealing on of the darkness, and then, as the darkness cleared away, he heard the loud cry of Christ, and saw His head fall on His breast in death. Then ensued the rumble of an earthquake and the sway of the ground when the three crosses reeled against the sky, like masts of a ship in a storm, the rock of Calvary snapped with an explosion, and was rent to an unknown depth; and at the same time the sepulchres shook, and there were many of them opened, and exposed the dead which lay within.

"If Thou be the Son of God," the Jews had shouted under the Cross, and the Centurion, disturbed in mind, said to himself, "Truly—this was the Son of God."

Seven witnesses were borne to Christ outside the circle of His disciples and Apostles.

The possessed man in the synagogue of Capernaum had proclaimed Him at the opening of His ministry. Again, He had been proclaimed by the man with the devils in the country of the Gadarenes. At the Feast of the Tabernacles the multitude had cried out, "Of a truth, this is the Prophet;" but others said, "This is the Christ." (S. John vii. 40, 41.) Claudia Procula, the wife of Pilate, had testified, so even had Pilate himself, to His righteousness. The penitent thief had acknowledged Him, and now, after His death, the Centurion professes his conviction.*

According to S. Luke, the Centurion said, "Certainly this was a righteous man." If he declared that Christ was the Son of God, he did not in those words express what we mean by them, for among the Greeks and Romans their

---

* As there are to be seven trumpets and seven vials as signs before the end of all things, so were there seven signs attending the death of Christ: the earthquake, the opening of the graves, the rending of the veil, the breaking of the threshold of the Temple, the extinction of the perpetual lamp, the darkness, and the cessation of the bleaching of the scarlet cord that bound the scapegoat.

gods were supposed to have often appeared on earth, and even to have left offspring on earth. Certain heroes, and some noble families, claimed to be descended from the gods. The Centurion went as far as his light allowed. He acknowledged that Christ suffered without being guilty, and that there was divinity in Him.

The rending of the rocks was symbolical of one fruit of the Cross of Christ. That has ever been potent to shake and rend the hardest hearts; hearts that have been stubborn, and have refused to receive Him, have been broken by Christ's cry and pierced by His Cross. And the opening of the graves is also figurative, for hearts have been opened, and all the dead and corrupt imaginings, thoughts, passions that have been sealed up therein have been revealed, and have poured forth their evil at the foot of the Cross.

And as the bodies of the Saints which slept arose, so the old spiritual life, the old graces, which in the sinner have died and gone into the dust, at the shaking of the earth by the arousing cry of Christ, have revived and come forth to new life. To the broken and contrite heart, opening itself in confession to God, and waking to a new spiritual life, the veil is rent asunder, that hides God from man, and access is accorded into the Holy of Holies, through—as the Apostle says—a new and living way, even His flesh, Who hung for us on the tree of shame.

III.

The Pierced Side.

S. JOHN XIX. 34.

"One of the soldiers with a spear pierced His side, and forthwith came thereout blood and water."

WE are told by S. John that "the Jews, because it was the preparation, that the bodies should not remain upon the cross on the Sabbath Day (for that Sabbath Day was an high day), besought Pilate that their legs might be broken, and that they might be taken away."

The next day was the Passover, and the sun was about to set, so that the festival was soon to begin. According to Roman custom criminals who had been crucified were left to linger on the cross sometimes for days. The Church historian Eusebius tells us of martyrs in Egypt who remained on their crosses till they died of starvation. But occasionally, rarely indeed, the Romans lit fires under the crosses to accelerate the death of those who hung on them.* Among the Jews, however, this was not lawful. Even at ordinary times, a criminal might not remain suspended after nightfall. Moses had ordered (Deut. xxi. 22-3) "If a man have

---

* Cicero, ad Quint. frat. i. 2, 2.

committed a sin worthy of death, and he be to be put to death, and thou hang him on a tree: his body shall not remain all night upon the tree, but thou shalt in any wise bury him that day."

Accordingly, when Joshua hanged the king of Ai, it was only till eventide; "and as soon as the sun was set, Joshua commanded that they should take the carcase down from the tree." (Josh. viii. 29.) And again, when Joshua took the seven kings in the battle of Gibeon, "he hanged them on five trees; and they were hanging upon the trees until the evening. And it came to pass at the time of the going down of the sun, that Joshua commanded, and they took them down off the trees, and cast them into the cave wherein they had been hid." (Josh. x. 27.)

The reason given by Moses for this order was that if a victim were thus left hanging it would be regarded as a defilement of the land. The order was given out of mercy. A criminal expiated his offence by his death. If his sufferings were protracted this was unnecessary barbarism. Especially monstrous would it be that whilst men slept peacefully in their beds, a poor wretch should be writhing through the hours of darkness shrieking curses, and crying with pain.

The Passover was drawing on, every moment saw the shadows lengthened and the sun nearing the Western Sea.

The Jews, not out of compassion, but out of alarm lest defilement should fall on their land were the crucified to remain hanging all that moonlit night, besought Pilate that their bones might be broken. That morning they would not enter the Judgment Hall for fear of pollution, and now they seek to expedite the death of the victims for the same reason.

Among the Romans the breaking of the limbs was one form of execution. Augustus ordered his privy secretary, Thallus, to be thus put to death, because he had divulged the contents of a despatch. Indeed the breaking of the limbs on a wheel was a common form of execution in Europe till the beginning of this century. Sentence was given for the breaking from below upwards, or from above downwards, according to the guilt of the criminal. If from below, the executioner with an iron bar broke first the ankles, then the knees, then the wrists, the elbows, and so on to vital parts; but if the sentence was from above downwards, then the first stroke fell across the breast, and at once destroyed life.

Such as were crucified could find release by death only. Even if taken down from the cross, and cared for, the unfortunate man could hardly recover. After the destruction of Jerusalem, Josephus saw among the Jews who were crucified on the road to Tekoa three of his friends.

He at once went to Titus, and implored him to spare their lives. Titus consented that they should be taken down from their crosses, but though they were shown the greatest care, two of them died the same night, and only one recovered. *

"Then came the soldiers, and brake the legs of the first, and of the other which was crucified with Him. But when they came to Jesus, and saw that He was dead already, they brake not His legs."

Death on the cross was attended with awful convulsions. The strain on the nails produced cramp, and then convulsions, as in lock-jaw. It was, therefore, marvellous to the soldiers to see the body of Jesus resting peacefully already, without any movement in it, whereas those of the thieves twitched, and were contorted.

"One of the soldiers with a spear pierced His side, and forthwith came thereout blood and water. And he that saw it bare record, and his record is true: and he knoweth that he saith true, that ye might believe. For these things were done that the Scripture should be fulfilled, A bone of Him shall not be broken. And again, another Scripture saith, They shall look on Him Whom they pierced."

At the very hour that the soldiers were breaking the legs of the malefactors, and passing by Jesus, Who was sus-

* Vita. 75.

pended between them, the priests in the Temple were preparing the lamb for the daily offering, and carefully avoiding the breaking of a single bone. The law then in force among the Jews was "Whosoever shall break a bone of the pure paschal lamb shall incur a penalty of forty stripes."*

Not only so, but in the offering of the sacrificial lamb in the Temple, the priest was required "to pierce the heart (of the lamb), and make its blood flow forth." †

So was the Lord, the true Lamb, fulfilling in small particulars the types in the Temple sacrifice. The Rabbis indeed knew and applied those words of Zechariah to the Messiah, "They shall look on Him Whom they pierced;" and yet such blindness has fallen upon them that they fulfil the prophecies, and accomplish the types of which their sacrifices were foreshadows, and refuse to see the accomplishment taking place before their eyes. One of their commentators on the words of the Prophet said, "This is spoken of Jehovah, Whom they will pierce, and Jehovah says it." ‡

As on that night the destroying angel had passed over the houses where was the sign of blood, and the paschal lamb was slain, but smote elsewhere, so now do these executioners pass over the true Lamb of God, and smite only those others crucified with Him.

* Pesakim vii. 11.   † Tamid iv. 2.   ‡ Succa f. 52, 1.

But one soldier with a spear pierced His side. The spear entered on the right side under the ribs, and in the thrust the head perforated the heart, and as he withdrew the spear, there issued after it a stream of blood and water.

The Old Testament was a covenant in blood, the New in water. Admission into the Old was by the shedding of blood in circumcision; admission into the New is by the sprinkling of water. As from our Lord's side both flowed, it shewed Him as the source of both covenants: that of blood, which ended in His blood-shedding, that of water, which was to last till He comes again.

It is curious that Jewish traditions, as old, no doubt, as the time of Christ, said that Moses smote the rock twice in the wilderness, and that from it flowed first blood, and then water. This rock, as S. Paul says, was the figure of Christ. (1 Cor. x. 4.)

Moreover, as when Adam slept, God took Eve from his side and presented her to Adam, so now the Second Adam sleeps on the Cross, and His side is opened, and from it issue water and blood; water by which man is regenerated and admitted into Christ's Church; blood, the eucharistic banquet whereby man's fellowship with Christ in His Church is maintained.

Thus we may regard these two streams as figuring the two

Sacraments, whereby the life of the Church is begun and maintained.

It has been argued that the death of Christ on the Cross took place through the rupture of the heart, or rather, of the division between the two cells, a phenomenon which is known to occur through excessive agony or sorrow of mind.

In the garden of Gethsemane our Lord endured mental anguish so intense that it caused the sweat of blood, which would be attended with violent palpitations of the heart. On the Cross the agony was renewed and intensified, accompanied by the physical sufferings of the mode of punishment. This combination of agony would induce such palpitation, that, reaching extreme acuteness, a rupture would ensue, and when the soldier's spear penetrated the heart, the mingled fluids would flow forth together.*

"Out of the heart," said our Blessed Lord, "proceed all evil thoughts, murders, adulteries." There is the source of all evil. By the piercing of His heart He expiated our sins of the heart, as by His pierced hands and feet He atoned for our sins of act, and by His thorn-crowned head He made reconciliation for our sinful thoughts. As evil springs from the heart of man, so from the heart of the Son of Man flows the fountain of healing for the cleansing of trans-

---

* Dr. Stroud, M.D., "Treatise on the Physical Cause of the Death of Christ." London, 1847.

gression. As in the heart of man is the source of weakness, so from the heart of the Son of Man issues that blood which is to strengthen us against temptation, and enable us to master its infirmity.

The streams are mingled. In vain does the blood of pardon flow unless by baptism we have been cleansed and admitted into the Church; and in vain are we baptized unless we go on to the participation of the precious blood which nourishes and sustains that spiritual life which was initiated in us by the water.

> "Spring, O well! thou living water,
>   Spring! let evil men deride,
> Spring abundant, mingled torrent
>   From the Saviour's side!
> Flow, O well! O Blood and Water,
>   Streams of sacramental grace,
> Purifying past transgression,
>   Present sin efface.
>
> Flow, O well! in fonts for ever
>   Is the crystal water stored;
> Flow, O well! on countless altars
>   Is the purple Blood outpoured." *

---

* Church Songs, No. 49. Skeffington, 1884.

IV.

The Descent from the Cross.

S. MATT. XXVII. 57, 58.

"*When the even was come, there came a rich man of Arimathea, named Joseph, who also himself was Jesus' disciple: he went to Pilate, and begged the body of Jesus.*"

S. LUKE gives a few further particulars. He says that Joseph was a Councillor, that he was a good and just man, and that he had not consented to the counsel and deed of those who had condemned and delivered up Jesus; that he himself waited for the kingdom of God. S. Mark adds that he went boldly into the presence of Pilate and craved the body of Jesus. "And Pilate marvelled if He were already dead: and calling unto him the Centurion, he asked him whether He had been any while dead." The words of S. Mark are couched in a figure of speech which condenses a conversation into a few words. Pilate asked if Jesus were yet dead. The Centurion answered that He was so. Then Pilate further asked whether He had been dead any length of time. When quite satisfied he gave consent that the body should be delivered over to Joseph.

We cannot say for certain, but it seems probable that

Nicodemus and Joseph were brothers, and the sons of Gorion. We know something of these two men from Jewish sources. Nicodemus lived to the destruction of Jerusalem, and was reduced from great wealth to extreme poverty. A poor woman was seen collecting straw from a dung-heap after the ruin of the city, that therewith she might feed her cow, and on being asked her name, she said that she was the daughter of the once wealthy Nicodemus. Nicodemus was not the original name of this man, which was Bonai, and he is spoken of by Jewish writers as a disciple of Jesus. He received the name of Nicodemus from a miracle wrought by his prayers. In a time of great drought he prayed, and rain came and filled the tanks of Jerusalem. Joseph Ben Gorion was murdered by the zealots in the streets of Jerusalem during the siege.

Joseph, we are told by the Evangelist, was a Councillor, that is, a member of the Sanhedrim; he came forth doubtless to his garden, which was close to the scene of crucifixion. As Nicodemus, for fear of the Jews, came to Jesus by night, so did Joseph, his brother, steal out in alarm and distress, and hide in his garden, peering over the wall, or through the half-closed door, at what took place hard by. But when the sun was darkened, and the rocks were rent, full conviction took hold of him, and instead of hiding, he came forth, and went into the city, and asked for the body of

Jesus. The Greek word employed shows us that Joseph was outside, and that he went into the town to make his request.

The request was not an extraordinary one. The Roman judges were accustomed to deliver up the bodies of malefactors to their friends and relatives, only paricides were denied a grave among their kin. It was not till later, under Diocletian, that the right of relatives to carry off and bury the dead who had suffered execution was further limited, and denied in cases of high treason.

This it is which lends so high an interest to the Roman catacombs, for by Roman law there was as full protection accorded to the graves of Christians as to heathen, and no more interference attempted in the burial of those who suffered sentence by a judge than in the case of the noblest senator, or member of the imperial family. It was not till late, that this liberty was restricted, consequently the earliest Christian tombs and catacombs in Rome were executed with far more richness and freedom than those of later date. *

Joseph plucked up courage at last, and went to ask for

---

* Quinctil vi. 9, 10, 21. "Cruces succiduntur, percussos sepeliri carnifex non vetat." Ulpian, Dig. xlviii., p. 24. "Corpora eorum qui capite damnantur, cognatis ipsorum neganda non sunt. — Corpora animadversorum quibuslibet petentibus ad sepulturam danda sunt." See Kraus, "Roma Sotteranea," Bk. i. c. 3.

the body. The soldiers were about to remove the dead from their crosses, probably they intended to saw through the crosses, cast them down, withdraw the nails, and fling the dead into one of those burial places, which the Jews had for malefactors. There were two of these, one for those who were executed with the sword or were hung on the tree, the other for those who were stoned to death, or burnt. The Sanhedrim would not allow those who had suffered these sentences to be laid in the tombs of their fathers till their flesh had mouldered away, only then might their bones be collected and laid in their family tombs. Another rule among the Jews was that the cross, or stone, or sword wherewith a criminal had been put to death, should be buried near him, but whether the Roman soldiers would comply with this rule we may well doubt; however, the Jews who sought to have this execution regarded as the result of the condemnation of their council, would doubtless see to the fulfilment of the precept. The story of S. Helena having discovered the cross on Calvary, though lacking all contemporary confirmation, is not in itself impossible or improbable.

It is not unlikely that at the entreaty of Joseph, and perhaps bribed by him, the soldiers did not touch the cross and body of Jesus after that His side had been pierced, though they set to work to throw down and remove for burial the bodies of the two thieves. Joseph had obtained what he asked, and he hastily " brought fine linen." He was attended by Nicodemus, who " brought a mixture of myrrh and aloes, about a hundred pounds weight." He and Nicodemus returned to Calvary, where in the meantime Mary the mother of Jesus, Mary Magdalene, Mary the mother of James and Joses, and also Salome, with S. John, the beloved disciple, kept guard.

Then Joseph took the body down, assisted, doubtless, by Nicodemus and those of the Apostles who were present. " Then took they the body of Jesus, and wound it in linen clothes with the spices, as the manner of the Jews is to bury."

The Jews were wont to use the linen strips wherewith the books of the law were rolled as bands for wrapping round the bodies of their dead. It was thought that the volumes of the law gave a sanctity to these wraps, which were eagerly sought, and highly esteemed for this purpose. But, of course, this was not possible for all, it was a privilege reserved for the few. The Jews did not suffer their dead to be enveloped in silk, or any embroidered stuff, only in white linen. The linen was in small strips, and was wrapped round and round the body, and the spices were inserted between the wraps and the body or in the folds of the linen. At the same time perfumes were burnt; and we are told that at the funeral of Gamaliel seventy pounds of spices were thus consumed.

On this occasion we are told that Nicodemus brought a mixture of myrrh and aloes a hundred pounds in weight. There is some difficulty about this, as the amount seems enormous, and it has been argued that the measure meant is only an eighth of a pound as we reckon it, so that the quantity brought by Nicodemus would not amount to more than twelve pounds, and this, perhaps, included the weight of the jar. Probably he brought an unopened vessel of the mixture and carried it to Calvary with him, and there broke it open, to use of it as much as might be required, or could be used in the hurry of the hasty entombment.

It is certainly remarkable that Joseph and Nicodemus, the two most timid, as it would seem, of Christ's disciples, should now show such boldness. One was His disciple, " secretly, for fear of the Jews," and the other was he who came " at the first, to Jesus by night." As they had been equal in the feebleness of their faith during the life of their Lord, so are they equally conspicuous for the boldness of their faith after His death.

What they now did was, indeed, a bold thing. It was a defiance of public opinion, it was the running the risk of expulsion from the synagogue, and from the high council. Although the entering of the court of justice carried with it defilement, Joseph went boldly before Pilate. He made a sacrifice of his popularity with his fellow councillors, and all the Pharisees and Scribes.

The example of these two men, Joseph and Nicodemus, is valuable. It shows us how that the grace of God can so act on the soul that a man will shake himself free from all his scruples, conquer his natural timidity, brave public opinion, sacrifice his favour with the people for the sake of Christ, to act conscientiously. There are turning points in all lives, critical moments when everything depends on momentary action. Probably this was such a critical moment in the lives of these two timid men. Had they hesitated, made excuses for themselves, justified their abstention from the last acts of mercy on the plea that they were not relatives, and not therefore morally bound to demand the body of Christ, then their after career would have been one of falling back into unbelief. But they acted on instant conviction; they rose to the emergency. The call came to do this act to the dead body of Him whom they had followed timidly in life, and they did not turn a deaf ear; they acted on what they thought to be right.

And lastly, we see from their conduct that God's grace is sufficient to conquer human weakness. When they had the will to do what was right, the grace of God came and strengthened them to fulfil that duty they saw they were called to perform.

V.

The Entombment.

S. LUKE XXIII. 53.

"He laid it in a sepulchre that was hewn in stone, wherein never man before was laid."

JOSEPH of Arimathea had a garden close to Calvary, and in that garden a new tomb. S. John mentions the garden, and the gate leading to Calvary was called the Garden Gate, because the road that passed through it traversed a number of gardens belonging to the wealthy citizens and councillors. A little below Calvary was the tank or pool of Gihon, from which the water was drawn for the gardens. Indeed, S. Cyril of Jerusalem, born in A.D. 315, speaks of the remains of garden enclosures about the Holy Sepulchre that were observable in his day.[*] In the garden of Joseph was a rocky face of the hill, in which he had had a new grave made, no doubt for himself, and that this was not the only one in that neighbourhood is shewn by the remains of old graves scooped out of the rock, still observable in the Church of the Holy Sepulchre.

The graves of well-to-do Jews consisted of an entrance

[*] Catech. xv. 5.

hall scooped out of the rock, in which was a stone table on which the embalming of the corpse might be carried out. Then came a round hole, closed with a circular stone slab that rolled, like a mill-stone, and within was the tomb proper—a chamber, with graves.

The body of Jesus was conveyed from the Cross to the ante-chamber of the tomb, and there washed, anointed, and wrapped round with the spices. According to Jewish law no woman might perform these last rites to the dead body of a man, they must be performed by men. Accordingly we are told that the women "followed after," that "Mary Magdalene and the other Mary" were "sitting over against the sepulchre." They would not dare to approach and assist, their place was at a distance. The office of women at an entombment was to utter lamentations over the dead.

Tombs about to be used, or in use, were whited over with lime, partly to give them a cheerful and glittering appearance, partly for sanitary purposes. But this grave was unwhitened, because it was used hurriedly without any preparation for its guest.

Among the Romans at the time it was customary to burn their dead, and lay up the ashes in urns in chambers erected to receive them. But in earlier times this was not the case, and some of the noble Roman families retained the earlier usage of burying their dead in sarcophagi, instead of burning them.* Among the Egyptians, the dead were embalmed, wound in linen, and buried in subterranean vaults; but the Jewish dead were not embalmed in the same way. The Egyptians opened their dead, removed the entrails, and filled the stomach with spices. The Jews merely wrapped unguents and spices about the bodies.

If we accept the tradition that the present Church of the Holy Sepulchre stands over the real grave of Jesus, then the distance from it to the place believed to have been that where the Cross stood is 110 feet. The original tomb was much interfered with by Constantine when he built the Church over it, but the vault of living rock remained till the Calif Hakim destroyed it in the year 1010.

Christ was laid in the grave at a distance of two hours' walk from Bethlehem. When He was born, it was in a cave, and now He is again laid in a cave. When He was taken to Jerusalem to the Temple, Simeon, a member of the Council, received Him in his arms, and now, as He is laid in His grave, a Councillor bears Him in his arms. Simeon had prophesied that He would be "a sign which would be spoken against," and his words had been fulfilled.

"And Mary Magdalene, and Mary the mother of Jesus,

*As in the tomb of the Scipios, and in that of the Nasones.

beheld where He was laid." "And they returned, and prepared spices and ointments: and rested the Sabbath Day, according to the Commandment." Christ had been nailed to the Cross at noon, and He had died at four o'clock. The sun must have been now rapidly setting, and after its golden disc had touched the sea, the Sabbath, the Paschal Feast, began, and no work might be done. The last offices were performed to Christ in haste; Joseph and Nicodemus did what they could in the short time they had at their disposal, but they intended to re-do the work more thoroughly when the Sabbath was over. They had no expectation of a resurrection; nor had the women who hastened home to prepare the mixture of myrrh, aloes, and cassia, for the ointment, and the gums that were to be burnt as a sweet incense on the Sunday. In the Temple, after the sacrifice of the bloody offering, came the oblation of incense; and so now, after the Sacrifice on Calvary was offered, came from the faithful men and women the oblation of sweet scents. At His birth, wise men had offered gold and frankincense and myrrh. There is now no present of gold, but of myrrh and of frankincense.

The women did not wring their hands, and utter loud wailing, tear their hair, and wound their faces, as is customary in the East at a funeral, for by Jewish law, one who had died as a criminal might not thus be noisily lamented. "If his relatives be in grief," it was commanded, "let them keep their grief locked up in the heart." When Jairus' daughter was dead, the house was at once filled with minstrels and professional wailers. It was not so now. In silence, broken only by the low, controlled sobs of the women, and the hushed whispers of the men, the Lord was laid in the tomb.

As already stated in the previous lecture, it was a rule among the Jews to bury with one who had been executed everything which had been used in putting him to death. Consequently, we may be sure that the two councillors would bring with them the nails and the crown of thorns, and lay them in the tomb with Jesus. It is also very probable that a lamp would be lighted and placed in the tomb. It was now the hour for the lighting of the Sabbatical lamp in each house; Joseph no doubt had his garden-house, or lodge, close by. It is remarkable that according to Jewish accounts the lamp in the Temple now went out. Did Joseph, at this hour for kindling the Sabbatical lamp, place one in the grave with Christ as extinction came on the Temple light?

In a garden man fell, and death came on man. In a garden Jesus was bowed in agony in prayer, and now in a garden He is laid dead. Out of the dust man was created, and now in the dust the second Adam is laid. As

Cain was moved with anger and envy against his brother and slew him, so now is this second Abel slain, and His blood cries from the ground against His murderers. In life Christ had not where to lay His head, and now in death He is given a borrowed grave.

Let us turn our eyes elsewhere, and we shall see on this same day another hanging on a tree, and falling therefrom to a horrible bursting asunder of his body. This is Judas, the traitor. He, filled with remorse, but not repentance, restores the thirty pieces of silver which he had taken as his pay for betraying his Master, casts them down in the Temple, and rushes forth to hang himself. The rope or the branch gives way, and the dead man, the suicide, is precipitated to the ground, and, no doubt, in order that the law may be observed, some who have discovered him, hastily, with averted faces, cover him over with the red clay from the Potter's field, where probably this act of suicide was committed. In the account given by S. Peter in the first chapter of the Acts, Judas had bought this field with the money he had received for the betrayal of Christ, and it received its name from his violent death in it. This is apparently at variance with the account of S. Matthew, according to which the field of blood was purchased by the priests with the thirty pieces of silver, after they had been cast down by Judas, as a burial-place for strangers. But the discrepancy is easily explained. Judas had made the agreement to take the field, and then before paying the sum was filled with horror, probably at the signs, the darkness, and the earthquake, and he went to the priests and threw down the money, then in his despair committed suicide in the field he had bought. Afterwards the priests, hearing of the contract, concluded it, and in the place where Judas had died, there thenceforth they buried strangers. The field is still pointed out, and is called Hak ed-damm; it lies on the steep southern face of the valley of Hinnom, near its eastern end, more than half way up the side.

The evening closes in; the golden sun has dipped into the sea, and night creeps on. Pilate sat down to his supper ill at ease with himself; the priests were in consternation at the rent veil; the soldiers probably alarmed by the earthquake. A vague alarm and unrest filled most hearts; those whose consciences were not shaken were troubled by the signs and wonders. And pure, calm, brilliant, the Paschal moon looks down on Jerusalem, and on two graves— fresh graves—that in Joseph's garden, and that in the Potter's field.

> "Let me hew Thee, Lord, a shrine
> In this rocky heart of mine,
> Where, in pure embalmèd cell,
> None but Thee may ever dwell.

> Myrrh and spices will I bring,
> True affection's offering;
> Close the door from sight and sound
> Of the busy world around;
> And in patient watch remain
> Till my Lord appear again."

NOTE: In Jewish graves, out of the inner apartment, or tomb proper, very generally open small oblong holes in the rock, into which the bodies were thrust, head or foot foremost. But this was not always the case, there were also sometimes graves cut out lengthways in the side, sometimes sarcophagi. The former (as in the tombs of the kings and of the Judges) were for the economization of space. That of Christ was certainly not of this sort, but probably the body was not laid in the final bed, but in the midst of the inner chamber.

VI.

The Great Sabbath.

S. LUKE XXIII. 56.

"They returned . . . and rested the Sabbath Day according to the Commandment."

THE religions of the heathen, with their myths and sacred rites, were to them schoolmasters, leading them to Christ; were to them, in an inferior manner, what the Law and Ceremonial of Moses were to the Jews.

There was a custom in Palestine, and in Asia Minor, and Egypt, which was a distant foreshadowing of the events of Good Friday, Easter Eve, and Easter Day. The story was told that a certain god, variously called Atys, Thammuz, and Osiris, had been cruelly and treacherously put to death; and in the early spring there was celebrated the day of the death of the god. Then garden graves were made for him and planted with flowers. On the second day the women wailed, to testify their sympathy with his mother, who sought him with tears, and on the third day they shouted for joy because he had been found, and was restored to life again.

And now He to Whom these rites had pointed, and pointed more distinctly than did any rite in the Jewish

Church, had been put to death, was laid in His garden grave, and His mother and the holy women spent the Sabbath that followed in weeping because of His loss. That had come to pass in reality which in the annual rites of Thammuz and Atys was but a fiction. As Christ fulfilled and took away the old Mosaic sacrifices, so He fulfilled these heathen typical ceremonies, and transformed them. Henceforth throughout the world there was to be celebrated the death day of the Lord of Life, and after that was to be observed a day of rest, in which He reposed in the grave, to be followed with a day of rejoicing at His victory over death.

"Now the next day that followed the day of the preparation," says S. Matthew, "the chief priests and Pharisees came together unto Pilate, saying, Sir, we remember that that deceiver said, while He was yet alive, After three days I will rise again: Command therefore that the sepulchre be made sure until the third day, lest His disciples come by night, and steal Him away, and say unto the people, He is risen from the dead: so the last error shall be worse than the first. Pilate said unto them, Ye have a watch, go your way, make it as sure as ye can. So they went, and made the sepulchre sure, sealing the stone, and setting a watch."

S. Matthew speaks of this Sabbath Day, the Paschal Feast, as the day after the Preparation. He no longer names the Paschal Feast, because that Paschal Feast is abrogated. The True Lamb has been slain, of which the lambs slain for the Passover were types.

The Jewish day began at sunset. It is a little uncertain whether S. Matthew is employing the Jewish or the Roman calculation of time, and so it cannot be said with certainty whether, when he says that the Jews asked to have the grave watched, they went on Friday evening after sundown, or on Saturday. It is hardly likely that they would make the request when the Paschal Sabbath festival had begun; it is most likely that they asked for the guard on Saturday evening, after the Sabbath rest was over. Then the shops would open, and people would be about in the twilight. The women bought spices, and mixed the ointments, and the priests set the watch and sealed the stone.

During the Saturday, doubtless, Pilate drew up his report of what had taken place, to send to the Emperor. This was done by all governors of provinces. Indeed, we know that from Alexandria a daily report of what took place was forwarded to Rome.* And these reports were preserved in the Roman archives. Eusebius, the Church Historian, asserts that Pilate actually did send such an account to the Emperor Tiberius, and so does Tertullian. The apologists

---

* These daily reports were called ὑπομνήματα καὶ ἐφημερίδες, commentarii rerum quotidianarum. Philo, legat. ad Caium. Euseb. Hist. Eccl. ii. 2; Tertull. Apol. c. 21.

had no scruple in appealing to the testimony of these Acts; they exhorted the Roman emperors to refer to them, and see if what the Christians asserted concerning Christ was not confirmed by the testimony of Pilate. The archives no doubt perished in the great conflagration of Rome under Nero. At all events they have not come down to us.*

The Jewish Council also, we are told by Justin Martyr, sent letters to all the synagogues, announcing the execution of Christ.

Apparently the Emperor was dissatisfied with what he heard, for the Jewish Council was thenceforth forbidden to assemble. We learn from Jewish authority that this was the case about forty years before the destruction of the Temple, but they give no reason for it; and we may without much hesitation believe that Pilate reported the tumult as occasioned by the sentence of the Sanhedrim, whereupon the Emperor forbade the Sanhedrim from again assembling and pronouncing sentence in spiritual cases even.

The watch set by the priests was the same Temple guard which was employed in the taking of Christ in Gethsemane. This guard was allowed to the Jews to protect the Temple from profanation, but they might not employ it outside the Temple precincts without permission from the Roman governor; this is why the priests approach Pilate with their

* The so-called Acts of Pilate are apocryphal.

request, and why he answers, "Ye have a watch." He gave them the requisite permission.

The soldiers set to guard the grave were Roman legionaries. The night was divided into watches, each soldier received a token on which was stamped the number of the watch he was to keep, and when the guard was changed, each of the soldiers relieved delivered up the token to the officer in charge. Roman guards were not allowed their shields, lest they should lean on them, and go to sleep. Doubtless the same rule held with the Temple guards. It is striking that now the watch kept on the Temple should be weakened, in order that part of it might be sent as a guard to Him Who rests in the grave, and has converted that into His Temple. There were four night watches, and a division of sixteen men was given charge over the grave, that is to say, there would be four sentinels at a time on duty.

The priests sealed the stone. That is to say they affixed wax to the *golal* or rolling circular stone that closed the opening into the inner chamber of the grave, drew a string through it and sealed again the stone in which the door was hewn. In like manner Darius (Dan. vi. 17) sealed the stone door that closed the lions' den; and we learn from profane history that, in like manner, did Alexander the Great seal the grave of Cyrus. To the present day in the Roman Catacombs we see how the early Christians, in their desire in all points to make their burials like to the entombment of Christ, closed the doors of their sepulchres hewn in the rock, with a stone, and sealed them—sometimes with rings and cameos, sometimes with the bottoms of gilded glass cups on which were engraved sacred subjects; and as Christ was laid with spices, so did they place little vessels in their graves that contained unguents and fragrant oils.*

On this evening the first fruits were brought into the Temple. The Sabbath being ended, there came a procession from the vale of Kedron, bearing the first sheaf of barley to the Temple, and this was received by the priests in the entrance of the Temple, and carried within. As the sheaf was presented the Levites in the gates sang Psalm xxx.—"I will magnify Thee, O Lord, for Thou hast set me up: and not made my foes to triumph over me;" to which the ascending procession sang in reply—"I profess this day unto the Lord my God, that I am come unto the country which the Lord sware unto our fathers for to give us." Then the priest took the first fruits and laid it before the altar, with the song, "A Syrian ready to perish was my father." (Deut. xxvi. 5-11.)

With this the harvest season was solemnly opened. We

---

* These are the so-called "vessels with the blood of martyrs." It is questionable whether martyr-blood is contained in any of them, it is certain that the vast majority contain nothing of the sort, but balsam.

shall see in the succeeding lecture what this signified, and how it was being carried out in a marvellous manner, by Christ.

So the great Sabbath, the day of rest, came to an end. Again the sun set, and again the Paschal moon poured its flood of silver light over the holy city, over Calvary and the Sepulchre. On the preceding night there had been perfect stillness in the garden. Twinkling lights had illumined the city, for all households were keeping the Passover.* Now it was different; four soldiers paced in the moonlight before the grave, and there was a hum of voices from the distant city. The pool of Gihon glittered in the moonlight like a silver plate, and the fig-trees cast dark shadows on the ground. The fireflies hovered about like floating stars. In the broad moonlight the nightingales in the garden trees sang, and the air was fragrant with the scent of the flowering acacias.

> "Calm Thou liest in the grave,
> With the virgin rock around;
> All is hush'd beneath the ground.

---

* I have assumed throughout that S. John's chronology is correct, and that Jesus died at the same time that the Paschal lambs were slain; that therefore He forestalled the Passover by a night. He died on the 14th Nisan; the 15th was the Passover, beginning on the eve, *i.e.* after sunset on the Friday.

The Great Sabbath.

All is dark, except the flare
From the lamp, in start and fall
Staining, with an ochreous glare,
    The napkin, and the pall.

Calm Thou liest! Thy pale hands
Folded o'er Thy pulseless breast.
Angels' burning lips are press'd
On each crimson print of nail,
As above the Mercy Seat
Angels' pinions form a veil
    About Thy Head and Feet.

Calm Thou liest! Thy pure brow
Marked with bulrush blow, and torn
By the ragged braid of thorn,
Still is crowned. Clotted flakes
Of Thy hair hang moisture full.
Thorns shall bloom, when morning breaks,
    Thy locks be white as wool.

Calm Thou sleep'st! The night fleets fast,
The hours are stealing on to morn,
The veil droops in the Temple, torn,
The moon is set, more deep the gloom,
The watch is changed about Thy prison;
But sudden! Light from out the tomb—
    The Lord! The Lord is risen!

VII.

The Spirits in Prison.

1 PETER III. 19.

"He went and preached unto the spirits in prison."

WE have come now to consider that very mysterious article of our Creed which we profess when we say of Jesus that after His death and burial "He descended into Hell." It is an article deserving of consideration, but it is one which it is impossible to understand aright unless we first investigate what was the belief of the Jews at the time of our Lord's death, relative to the Spirit World. And this is the more advisable, as in our Blessed Lord's teaching He adopts the phraseology of His contemporaries, and therefore confirms their teaching, at least in its broad outlines.

The Jews held that there was a place of "outer darkness," which they called Gehenna, where were flames and the undying worm, where were "wailing and gnashing of teeth." This was regarded as the place of the utterly lost. It is the same as our Hell, but is not the same as the Hell of the Creed. Above Gehenna was, according to the Jews, another region called Sheol, deep and dark, and a prison. Between

Sheol and Paradise flows a river of fire, in which those who have contracted defilement during life, but are generally righteous, pass, and are cleansed before they enter Paradise. But Paradise, again, is only the outer court of the Heavenly Temple, a place not of perfect bliss, but of expectation of the Messiah, Who alone can bring the souls of the faithful into perfect felicity in the immediate presence of God.

Such were the divisions of the World of Spirits according to Jewish belief. Now our Lord named all three; He spoke of Gehenna repeatedly; it is named seven times by Him in S. Matthew's Gospel, beside other references to it without being named, but as the place of outer darkness, where is weeping and gnashing of teeth. Sheol, or Hades, is twice named in S. Matthew's Gospel, and in S. Luke's Dives is said not to be in Gehenna, but in Sheol, and we might even suppose he were in the purifying river of fire of Jewish belief were we not told that there was no passing from the one place to the other.

According to the belief of the Jews the faithful dead were in earnest expectation of the Messiah, Who would release them and place them in the full glory of the presence of God. So they interpret the wonderful passage of Isaiah (xxxv. 8, 9), "He will swallow up death in victory; and the Lord God will wipe away tears from off all faces; and the rebuke of His people shall He take away from off all the earth. And it shall be said in that day, Lo, this is our God; we have waited for Him, and He will save us: this is the Lord; we have waited for Him, we will be glad and rejoice in His salvation." These words are said to refer to the Messiah releasing the spirits of the just from their place of expectation. Elsewhere the Jewish Rabbis say that the Son of David would pass through this place of departed spirits and deliver those therein; and they apply to this the words of the Prophet Hosea—"I will ransom them from the power of the grave (of Sheol); I will redeem them from death: O death, I will be thy plague; O Sheol, I will be thy destruction." (xiii. 14.) And also that promise in Zechariah, "By the blood of Thy Covenant I have sent forth Thy prisoners out of the pit wherein is no water. Turn you to the stronghold, ye prisoners of hope: even to-day do I declare that I will render double unto thee." (ix. 11, 12.)

Now if we consider what was the belief in our Lord's time, not only as to the places occupied by the departed, but also as to the dead being in expectation of deliverance by the Messiah, Who is the Son of David, and Who is One with Jehovah,* then I think it is not hard to understand the

---

* Echa Rabbati, f. 59. "What is the Name of Messias? Abba Ben Cahana replied, His Name is Jehovah, for it is written, His Name shall be called, The Lord our Righteousness."

event of Easter Eve, and to understand the allusions to it in the New Testament writers. S. Peter says that Christ went down and preached to the spirits in prison, in Sheol; and then he mentions those that were disobedient at the time of the flood. The reason for this is that the Jews expressly denied the possibility of salvation by the Messiah to those who were overwhelmed by the flood, as well as to certain others;* now S. Peter singles out this group of souls to which the Jews denied redemption, to say that Christ did go down and carry pardon and give release even to them. His words may thus be paraphrased. "After Christ suffered in the flesh, His spirit went down into Sheol, and preached pardon to all those there, even to those to whom you deny happiness—such as were disobedient in the days of Noah."

Now we can see that the prophecy, "The people which sat in darkness saw great light; and to them which sat in the region and shadow of death light is sprung up," had a further reference than to those in the borders of Zebulon and Napthali; and how that the words of Zacharias in the Benedictus may have had a special reference to the souls in Sheol. "The dayspring from on high hath visited us, to give light to them that sit in darkness and in the shadow of

---

* Sanhed, c. 11, 3. "Those who perished in the Flood shall have no lot in the world to come."

death, to guide our feet into the way of peace," may have referred to the release of spirits of the dead as well as to the spiritual enlightenment of the living. When Christ declared that His mission was "to preach deliverance to the captives," it was not only deliverance in this life to those held captive of Satan, but also to those "prisoners of hope" who, said the Prophet, were to obtain release "by the blood of the covenant."

The ancient patriarch Jacob, when dying, in his prophetic song exclaimed, "I have waited for Thy salvation, O Lord." (Gen. xlix. 18.) David, in a moment of doubt, asked, "Shall the dead rise up again and praise Thee? Shall Thy lovingkindness be showed in the grave: or Thy faithfulness in destruction?" (Ps. lxxxviii. 10, 11.) But Isaiah answered with confidence, "Thy dead men shall live, together with my dead body shall they arise. Awake and sing, ye that dwell in the dust"—only they must be content for awhile to "enter into" their "chambers" hewn in the rock, and "hide" themselves "as it were for a little moment, until the indignation be overpast." (xxvi. 20-1.)

And now let us look at the ceremony that was taking place on the Saturday evening in Jerusalem. A first sheaf of barley was cut in the vale of Kedron, and was brought up the hill by the greatest among the people; when there was a king among them, by a king, on his shoulder, in a basket. It was received by the priests and Levites at the Temple gates, with songs of praise; and the bearer said, "A Syrian ready to perish was my father, and he went down into Egypt and sojourned there; and the Egyptians evil entreated us, and afflicted us, and laid upon us hard bondage, and when we cried unto the Lord God of our fathers, the Lord heard our voice, and looked on our affliction, and our labour, and our oppression: and the Lord brought us forth out of Egypt with a mighty hand, and with an outstretched arm—and He hath brought us into this place, and hath given us this land, even a land that floweth with milk and honey."

We see now how significant this was of the great deliverance being wrought by Christ, Who went down into the valley of the shadow of death, and thence now brought up the first fruits—not the fine wheat of the new Covenant, the wheat of His harvest field the Church, but the barley of the old Covenant, the harvest field just ripe of the Jewish synagogue. And we see now how significantly the great going forth by night out of Egypt was, of this great going forth out of the pain of bondage in Sheol, after the slaying of the Paschal lamb.

Now, also, we can understand what the Church means when she gives us as the first lesson for Easter Eve the prophecy of Zechariah, and for the first lesson on Easter

Day the 12th Chapter of Exodus, and we can see the fulness of signification of these words, "It is a night to be much observed unto the Lord for bringing the people out from the land of Egypt: this is that night of the Lord to be observed of all the Children of Israel in their generation." We see how that that first deliverance was a type of the still mightier deliverance that would be wrought by the Prophet "like unto Moses;" and how that the commemoration of that deliverance was not only to the Jew a looking back on what had been done in the past, but a yearly encouragement to look forward to what would be done for him by the Messiah in the future.

It was customary in the Middle Ages on Easter Eve for nobles and great men to visit the hospitals and leper houses and the orphanages, and to give alms; and in Russia, I believe, to the present day, at all events, till recently, on Easter Eve the Czar or Grand Duke visits the prisons and gives to the prisoners some words of consolation and hopes of release. These acts are, or were, commemorations of the descent of Christ into the prison-house of Spirits.

Are not we also, in a way, here on this earth, " prisoners of hope?" *Prisoners*, indeed, we are; tied and bound with the chains of sin and bad habits; in darkness also, away from the light of God's presence.

But, also, prisoners of *hope*, with the glorious prospect

before us of release from the bondage here and admission to the glorious liberty of the Children of God in the land of rest and peace. And as the old patriarchs were set free from their prison-house by the Blood of the Covenant, so are we. Through the precious Blood of Jesus alone we receive remission of sin and release from the slavery of Satan. And as the Prophet exhorted the Jews, "Turn unto your stronghold, ye prisoners of hope," so may we be addressed. Christ is our stronghold; a very present help in time of trouble. If to Him we turn in distress, in temptation, when galled with our chains; to Him Who preaches deliverance to captives; to Him, our stronghold; then He will release us, and make true His word to us as to the old patriarchs who expected release—" Even to-day will I restore double unto you."

VIII.

The Resurrection.

S. MATT. XXVIII. 2-4.

"Behold, there was a great earthquake: for the angel of the Lord descended from Heaven, and came and rolled back the stone from the door, and sat upon it. His countenance was like lightning, and his raiment white as snow: and for fear of him the keepers did shake, and became as dead men."

CHRIST is risen! He has broken the gates of death and snapped the bars of iron in sunder. O death, where is thy sting! O grave, where is thy victory?

Now is sorrow ended and joy come. Heaviness has endured for a night, now, in the morning, cometh rejoicing. Christ is risen, and as He rises "many bodies of the Saints which slept" arise also, and appear in the holy city.

There had been an earthquake when His soul left the body, there is an earthquake as it returns and re-animates it. Fear fell on the Jews at the first earthquake, when the graves were opened, and fear doubtless fell on them now on Easter morning as forth from the graves issue those who had fallen into dust and appear in the streets of Jerusalem. Indeed, such an impression did this resurrection of the dead Saints leave on men's minds that S. Paul had to combat the doctrine founded on it by Hymenæus and Philetus that the Resurrection was passed already. (2 Tim. ii. 18.)

Christ is the first fruits of them that slept, the first to rise, and He raises with Him some of the dead in pledge of a future general resurrection harvest. "God hath raised Him up, having loosed the pains of death: because it was not possible that He should be holden of it. . . . Therefore did my heart rejoice," said David, "and my tongue was glad; moreover also my flesh shall rest in hope." (Acts ii. 24, 26.) Henceforth "Blessed are the dead which die in the Lord." (Rev. xiv. 13.) The doctrine of the Resurrection, that as Christ was raised, so also will all those that sleep in Christ be raised, was the cardinal point of the preaching of the Apostles. "If Christ be not risen," said S. Paul, "then is our preaching vain, and your faith is also vain. If the dead rise not, then is not Christ raised: and if Christ be not raised, your faith is vain; ye are yet in your sins."

What said the heathen?

> "Suns may set and rise again,
> Light by us is sought in vain,
> When we enter death's domain.
> Then we pass to endless night,
> Hope for e'er has taken flight,
> Never dead returned to light."—*(Catullus.)*

Pliny in his Natural History says that the expectation of resurrection is a folly; and when S. Paul preached the Resurrection in Athens, men mocked. In former times men had some belief in the continuance of life after death, and perhaps some dim fluttering hope of a resurrection; but in our Lord's time all trust in a future had died away, and even among the Jews the whole sect of the Sadducees denied that there was any resurrection. This was not so among the Pharisees. They looked for a restoration of all things, and that through the Messiah.*

"Mary Magdalene, and Mary the mother of James, and Salome, had brought sweet spices, that they might come and anoint Him. And very early in the morning the first day of the week, they came unto the sepulchre at the rising of the sun." (S. Mark xvi. 1, 2.) S. Matthew says they started "as it began to dawn towards the first day of the week." S. Luke says "very early in the morning." S. John also uses the same expression. S. Luke does not mention Salome, and S. John does not mention Mary the mother of James.

* Sohar in Gen. f. 85. "When the Messiah shall have risen, then shall Jacob enter on the possession of earthly and heavenly goods." In Exod. f. 23. "Those who went out of Egypt with Moses shall rise again in their bodies as witnesses." Midrash Mishle, f. 53. "Why is Messiah called Jinon? (Ps. lxxii. 17.) Because He will raise up from the dust all that sleep in it." Jalkut Simoni, f. 56. "Our Rabbis teach that at the coming of Messiah, in the month Nisan, our forefathers shall rise and exclaim, O Messiah! Thou Lord, our Righteousness."

The Resurrection.

It is worthy of remark that not one of the Evangelists describes to us the manner in which Christ rose, but they tell us only of the evidences that the grave had been deserted. All of them record the event, and give us every assurance that as He suffered under Pontius Pilate so did He also rise the third day from the dead. They state the fact, but give no account of it. Christ had risen amidst the darkness of the night without breaking the seals or removing the stone. It was not till after He had risen that the angel descended and rolled away the stone in order that soldiers keeping watch and disciples alike might see that the grave was empty.

The angel came down from Heaven in splendour, and the stone was removed from the entrance of the grave. The keepers did shake and became as dead men, and fled into the city, and told the priests what had taken place. These they found in the Temple engaged on grinding the new corn brought in the night before, and making of it a cake with oil, that it might be offered before the Lord, after the new sheaf had first been lifted up and waved before the Lord in the Temple. Then "when they were assembled, with the elders, and had taken counsel, they gave large money unto the soldiers, saying, Say ye, His disciples came by night, and stole Him away while we slept. And if this come to the governor's ears, we will persuade him, and secure you.

So they took the money, and did as they were taught." S. Matthew adds that at the time when he wrote, "This saying is commonly reported among the Jews until this day." And later we have the evidence of Justin Martyr, of Tertullian and of Eusebius, that this belief prevailed among the Jews. Still later we have the same falsehood repeated in the profane Toledoth Jeshu, a life of Christ in circulation among the Jews, composed some time in the Middle Ages, which embodies their traditions concerning Christ. In it is related that Judas stole the body, diverted a stream that flowed through his garden, buried the body of Christ in the watercourse, and turned the river back into its bed again.

"The angel said to the women," when they arrived before the sepulchre, and with much amazement saw it open, and the angel seated on the stone, "Fear not ye: for I know that ye seek Jesus, which was crucified. He is not here: for He is risen, as He said. Come, see the place where the Lord lay. And go quickly, and tell His disciples that He is risen from the dead; and behold, He goeth before you into Galilee; there shall ye see Him: lo, I have told you."

The women knew nothing of a guard being set over the grave; probably one reason why the angel appeared and drove away the watch before they arrived was to protect

The Resurrection.

them from insult and mockery from these rude soldiers; and is a token to us how the Lord thought of and cared for these faithful women, in the midst of the glory of His Resurrection. The lightning blaze of the angel's countenance was to dismay and send the soldiers in panic from the tomb, but then its splendour faded, and the women do not appear to have been dazzled by it.

"And they departed quickly from the sepulchre, with fear and great joy; and did run to bring His disciples word. And as they went to tell His disciples, behold Jesus met them, saying, All hail. And they came and held Him by the feet, and worshipped Him. Then said Jesus unto them, Be not afraid: go tell My brethren that they go into Galilee, and there shall they see Me."

The women are four—Mary the mother of James, Joanna the wife of Chuza, Salome, and the Magdalene, and the last apparently outran the others, or they divided in search of the Apostles, and she found Simon Peter and S. John, and "saith unto them, They have taken away the Lord out of the sepulchre, and we know not where they have laid Him."

There is some difficulty in harmonising the several accounts, but the simplest is this. The four women came to the sepulchre, and when Magdalene saw that it was open, she at once ran back to the town—leaving the other three at the sepulchre, who then saw the vision of angels, and as they also returned to the city¹ were met by their risen Lord. Mary Magdalene had neither seen the angels nor the risen Saviour, for she says nothing about either. Then Peter and John run to the sepulchre, and she also follows, and stands weeping without, when the Lord appears also to her. If we take events to have happened thus, the difficulties disappear.

" Peter therefore went forth, and that other disciple, and came to the sepulchre. So they ran both together: and the other disciple did outrun Peter, and came first to the sepulchre. And he, stooping down and looking in, saw the linen clothes lying; yet went he not in. Then cometh Simon Peter following him, and went into the sepulchre, and seeth the linen clothes lie, and the napkin that was about His head not lying with the linen clothes, but wrapped together in a place by itself. Then went in also that other disciple, which came first to the sepulchre, and he saw, and believed. For as yet they knew not the Scripture, that He must rise again from the dead."

S. John was the youngest of the Apostles, and S. Peter the oldest, which will explain how he outran Peter. He stood in the vestibule of the tomb, the outer chamber, where was the stone table for embalming. He stooped and looked through the round opening into the tomb itself, an opening which was only large enough for a man to pass through stooping or crawling. But S. Peter crept through, and was then followed by S. John, and both convinced themselves that the grave was deserted.

We must not be surprised at their not understanding our Lord's words teaching His Resurrection, for they gave them a different signification to what He meant them to convey. According to the belief of their times, after death the soul remained near the body, and hovered to and fro by the head till the third day, on which, convinced that return was impossible, it rose to the spirit realm. Now when the disciples heard Jesus speak about His rising again the third day, they thought He meant that after His death, on the third day His soul would mount to Paradise; that He was only confirming the prevalent belief, or superstition. They could not imagine that He meant that the soul would re-animate the body, and raise it.

Not without deep significance did our Blessed Lord at His Resurrection leave behind Him the linen clothes and the napkin that was about His head, not lying with the linen clothes, but wrapped together in a place by itself. It was intended as a lesson of order and neatness. In the moment of Resurrection, of victory over death, He did not forget that orderliness is an obligation, and to shew this to be a duty—an important duty of Christianity, He made His grave neat before He left it. That was the sermon that the grave preached—the first lesson of Easter—[1]that slatternliness is inconsistent with Christianity.

Christ is risen! The first fruits of them that sleep. In the Temple this day the priest announces that the Harvest has begun, and he waves the offering of the first fruits before God. Christ is risen! He, our Great High Priest, presents before the Father the first sheaf of the ancient dead who fell asleep in faith. And see! how ever since the harvest has been going on. How the ears have fallen in the fields of the world; but though fallen yet they will be gathered in order, sheaf by sheaf, by Christ, and brought into the garner of the Lord—the temple not made with hands, eternal in the Heavens.

IX.

The Appearance to Mary Magdalene.

S. JOHN XX. 11.
"And Mary stood without the sepulchre, weeping."

THERE is, as already said, some difficulty at first sight in reconciling the accounts of the events of Easter morning as given by the four Evangelists, but the sequence seems to be this—The women, Mary Magdalene, Mary the mother of James, Joanna (S. Luke xxiv. 10), and Salome (S. Mark xxi. 1), came early to the sepulchre. Whether they all came together is not certain; if Mary Magdalene came separately from the others, much of the difficulty disappears.

According to S. John's account Mary Magdalene, who alone is mentioned by him, came early to the sepulchre, and finding the stone rolled away, ran and told Simon Peter, who along with S. John hastened to the tomb, and finding it empty returned to their lodgings in great perplexity. Mary Magdalene, however, remained outside the sepulchre weeping: "and as she wept, she stooped down, and looked into the sepulchre, and seeth two angels in white, sitting, the one at the head, and the other at the feet, where the body of Jesus had lain. And they say unto her, "Woman, why weepest thou? She saith unto them, Because they have taken away my Lord, and I know not where they have laid Him." After which Jesus Himself appeared to her.

S. Matthew and S. Mark say that the women all saw an angel, who bade them go and tell the disciples, and as they went Jesus appeared to them. Here also there is a difference, for S. Mark says that our Lord appeared first of all to Mary Magdalene, and makes no mention of the appearance to the other women.

S. Luke's account again differs. The women, Magdalene among them, came "very early" to the sepulchre, they see two angels, and after that S. Peter hastens to the tomb; and departs wondering.

It is most likely that the division of the parties, Mary Magdalene coming separately from the others, may explain, to some extent, the apparent difficulties.

As in the Tabernacle two cherubim spread their wings over the mercy-seat of the Ark, so now do two angels in white occupy the head and foot of the place where the body of Jesus had rested. They are there though Jesus has risen, and their presence seems to teach us that sanctity attaches to holy places, that, for instance, a Church in which the presence of Jesus has been, an Altar on which the Blessed Sacrament of His body and blood has reposed, are hallowed, not only at the moment of His presence, but remain consecrated, and are not to be treated with irreverence.

Mary had remained without, that is, in the porch of the grave, in a rocky vestibule, in which, as already explained, the embalming of corpses took place. John and Peter had retired; when they had gone, she timidly, weeping, entered this vestibule, but still stood " without," that is, outside the sepulchre proper. Then she stooped down, and looked into the inner chamber through the low, round hole, about three feet high, and then saw the angels. The ordinary pictures of the Resurrection confuse our ideas, or rather mislead them, and create for us difficulties which disappear when we come to consider the Gospel story according to what we know were the usages of the time.

"And when" Mary had said that she knew not where the Lord had been laid, "she turned herself back, and saw Jesus standing, and knew not that it was Jesus."

Objection has been made to this, that Mary should not have recognized Him, at a time when there must have been full morning light. But this objection ceases to have any force when we realize where Mary was, and how Jesus appeared to her. She was within the vestibule, opening into the garden by a door not closed at all. She was close to the inner, circular opening, that admitted into the tomb itself. She heard a step behind, and turned sharply round, and saw a figure occupying the door and obscuring the light and the sight of the garden. The fact of His standing there cut off the light, and so His face was dark against the brilliant morning sunshine which streamed in behind. Under the circumstances she could not distinguish His features, she could see only a dark figure of a man set in a golden light; and when He said unto her "Woman, why weepest thou? whom seekest thou?" it was natural that she should suppose Him to be the gardener. Very probably, under the hollow arched vault, His voice sounded differently from usual when He spoke under the open sky, or she may have been so bewildered by the vision of angels, and by her surprise at seeing someone entering the tomb behind her, that she did not recognize the tones of the voice she loved.

"She, supposing Him to be the gardener, saith unto Him, Sir, if Thou have borne Him hence, tell me where Thou hast laid Him, and I will take Him away."

It would seem that Joseph of Arimathea had a gardener's lodge connected with the garden, in which dwelt the keeper of the garden. Mary may have known this, and thought that this man was on his rounds, and had come in to see why she trespassed. In passing, we may observe that it was by no means unusual for tombs to be in gardens. We read of Manasseh that he "slept with his fathers, and was buried in the garden of his own house, in the garden of Uzza." (2 Kings xxi. 18.)

Observe the tender love, the fervour of piety in Mary, that impels her to offer to do more than she is able. She asks where Christ is laid, and will herself open His grave, and carry His dead body in her arms away. Could she have done this? Most certainly not; but in her love and distress she resolves to try to do it. Surely a lesson for us, who are always shrinking from duties, doubting our own powers, or rather excusing ourselves from attempting things by the plea of weakness. But when Mary thought that profane hands had possession of the Sacred Body, that it was subjected to unworthy treatment, she made no account of her weak woman's arms, of her little strength, of her being alone, she thought only of the dishonour done to her Lord. "Tell me where Thou hast laid Him, and I will take Him away." So, in the Song of Solomon, the Bride cries, "I sought him whom my soul loveth, I sought him, but found him not. I will rise now, and go about the city; in the streets, and in the broad ways, I will seek him whom my soul loveth: I sought him, but I found him not."

There perhaps ensued a pause after the question to Mary. Her eyes were full of tears—she had been weeping. Her heart was beating with alarm and distress. In that lull she wiped her eyes, and looked up intently at Him Who stood in the doorway, with the golden morning light behind Him—there was something in the outline of His form, something in His posture, something in the attitude of His uplifted hands, that made her heart stand still with a sudden expectation and awe. "Jesus saith unto her, Mary. She turned herself, and saith unto Him, Rabboni; which is to say, Master." Either, after having spoken first, she had reverted to her former position, and now turned again, which is unlikely, or this turning to Jesus, as He addresses her by name, is rather that of working herself up to Him on her knees. She had been kneeling, and had crouched to look into the inner vault; then she turned right round to speak to Him Whom she thought was the gardener, and now, probably, by this turning to Him is meant that she struggled to reach Him on her knees, that she might clasp His feet.

"Mary!" He said to her. He Who telleth the number of the stars, and calleth them all by their names, knows also the names of those who are stars in the firmament of His Church. Mary Magdalene was but a fallen star, who by grace had been raised, and purified by tears, and rekindled by great love, had been set again in the place whence she had lapsed. With a look Jesus had recalled Peter to a consciousness of himself, and by a word now He brings full conviction to Mary that it is He Himself Who stands before her. She, in her ecstacy of joy, would have clasped His knees, as Abigail kneeling before David, as the Shunammite before Elisha. But—"Jesus saith unto her, Touch Me not; for I am not yet ascended to My Father; but go to My brethren, and say unto them, I ascend unto My Father, and your Father, and to My God, and your God."

That "touch Me not" was a check administered to too exuberant and irreverent piety, and is a lesson not to be neglected at any time. The angels stood at the head and foot of the spot where the body of Jesus had lain, and shew us that places are hallowed, and to be treated with reverence, where Christ has been, and now Jesus shews that He Himself is to be reverently approached, and that the tenderest love, the most ardent devotion, must never transcend the limits of proper respect.

When God appeared on Sinai, barriers were set round the mount lest the Israelites should approach too near, and with light heart, and there are barriers about all the manifestations of God that must not be cast down or overleaped.

This is too often forgotten in these days, both by preachers in their addresses, and by worshippers in their prayers and hymns. The gross familiar style and the mawkish sentimental style are alike unsuitable. "If," said an Indian one day to a Wesleyan missionary, "I were to speak to my earthly prince in the way you address your God, he would have me expelled his presence."

In the Song of Songs the Bride says, "It was but a little that I passed from" the watchmen, "but I found him whom my soul loveth: I held him, and would not let him go."

But the Magdalene was not to touch Jesus, for "I am not yet ascended to My Father." He implies that after that event, she—and so others as well—might touch Him, might lay hold of Him, and "not let Him go." And, indeed, so is it. When Christ had ascended into Heaven, then began the Sacramental approach, and the Sacramental laying hold of Him. That which was not permissible to Mary, when Christ stood before her visibly, is permissible now that He is seen by faith, and the hands may now be extended to clasp Him, when He comes to us veiled in Sacramental forms.

X.

The Way to Emmaus.

S. MARK XVI. 12.

"*After that He appeared in another form unto two of them, as they walked, and went into the country.*"

WHAT S. Mark gives briefly, that is more fully told by S. Luke, who says, "And behold, two of them went that same day to a village called Emmaus, which was from Jerusalem about threescore furlongs."

This Emmaus was the Mozah mentioned in Joshua (xviii. 25),* of which the Talmud says, "Below Jerusalem is a little place called Mosa, whither men went to cut withies for the feast of the Tabernacles." It was afterwards called Colonieh, because after the fall of Jerusalem a Roman colony of soldiers was settled there.† The name Mosa means Pass, Emmosa—*the* Pass, and it is on the main road to the sea at Jaffa. The only difficulty attending this identification is the distance, which is forty-five furlongs instead of sixty; and the tradition, which is not very well authenticated as old, of its being at a place now called

---

* Cf. 1 Chron. viii. 36, 37; ix. 42.

† Joseph. Bell. Jud. vii. 6, 6. "Emmaus, which is distant from Jerusalem 60 stadia."

Kubêbe, which is actually situated at the right distance from the city. As, however, the Emmaus of Josephus is undoubtedly Colonieh, and he gives the same distance as S. Luke, we may conclude that the distance was reckoned somewhat roughly. Emmaus lies in a pleasant valley, and is imagined to have been the scene of the conflict between David and Goliath. The two disciples who lived at Emmaus were Cleopas and another, unnamed. Cleopas was not the Cleopas, or Alphæus, of the Gospel, but was probably a Greek Jew, and his full name was Cleopater.

As the two walked home from the festival of the Passover they had attended in Jerusalem, "they talked together of all those things which had happened."

It was towards evening, and the distance a walk of about an hour and a half. They went westward, along the road that twists about as it descends into the valley, and the evening sun shone in their faces.

"And it came to pass, that, while they communed together and reasoned, Jesus Himself drew near, and went with them. But their eyes were holden, that they should not know Him."

The way was narrow. It had traversed a very bare, mountainous, rocky soil, and now the fertile valley, with its olives and willows by the watercourse, opened before them.

They walked in the narrow way, one behind the other, or perhaps side by side, and they heard a Stranger pacing behind them. They did not turn to look at Him; the evening sun shone in their eyes, and dazzled them.

"And He said unto them, What manner of communications are these that ye have one with another, as ye walk, and are sad? And the one of them, whose name was Cleopas, answering said unto Him, Art thou only a stranger in Jerusalem, and hast not known the things which are come to pass there in these days? And He said unto them, What things? And they said unto Him, Concerning Jesus of Nazareth, which was a prophet mighty in deed and word before God and all the people."

The two disciples supposed that Jesus was one of the proselytes, or a foreign Jew who had come to the feast, and was like them returning. At the conclusion of the feast, the roads were full of people leaving; but as Cleopas and the other disciple lived at Emmaus, they had started on their walk home at a later time of day than those who were going further, so that probably at this time the road was not full of travellers.

Christ walked either just behind the two disciples or at their side, where the turf becomes covered with marigolds and chrysanthemums. He listened as they told Him how that He they had trusted would have redeemed Israel had been crucified, and how "certain women also of our company made us astonished, which were early at the sepulchre; and when they found not His body, they came, saying that they had also seen a vision of angels, which said that He was alive."

Then Jesus said to them, "O fools, and slow of heart to believe all that the Prophets have spoken! Ought not Christ to have suffered these things, and to enter into His glory? And beginning at Moses, and all the Prophets, He expounded unto them in all the Scriptures the things concerning Himself."

He began from where Moses tells of the prophecy that the Seed of the Woman should crush the Serpent's head, which would also bite the heel of the Son of Man. He shewed how that the Prophet spoken of by Moses like unto him, had indeed been raised up. He shewed how that David had described the sufferings of the Messiah, and the Prophets His birth, His mission, and His death and resurrection.

"And they drew nigh unto the village whither they went: and He made as though He would have gone further." They had reached the bridge that crosses the torrent in the Wady Hanina, and He made as though about to pursue His way through the deep cleft road to Arimathea, but there is at this point a side path leading right to the village of Emmaus, which lies on a height. Here it was, as the two turned out of the high way, that they saw their mysterious companion take some steps forward along the main road, westwards. Then—"they constrained Him, saying, Abide with us: for it is toward evening, and the day is far spent. And He went in to tarry with them."

Our Lord "made as though He would go further," indeed He took some steps in the course along the main road, and unless the two disciples had urged Him to tarry with them, He would have gone on. We see in this how opportunities arise and must be seized—how in spiritual as in temporal matters the secret of success is found in readiness to lay hold of an opportunity. The hesitating man, the man who takes a long time to make up his mind, very often misses chances.

The two disciples acted on the impulse of the moment, or the voice of conscience when it spoke, and were honoured with being permitted to extend hospitality to the Lord of Life. We see how man's free will plays a great part in the mystery of salvation. Christ accompanies man on his journey through life, but Christ will not take up His abode with man, and reveal Himself wholly to him, unless he, by an exercise of free will, "constrains" Him to abide with him. God often seems to us to make as though He were departing, or leaving us to ourselves, or even as if He had deserted us, when all the time He is¹ at our side, only waiting to be entreated to enter in and take up His abode in us. To the Children of Israel of old it seemed that God had abandoned them when Pharaoh increased the burden of their tasks, and made their lives heavy with hard bondage; yet then He was near to them, and was ready to draw them from the midst of the house of bondage. Let us, for our encouragement, remember that, when faith seems to fade, and when we most feel our loneliness, then is the time when we must use an exercise of free will, and by our urgency "constrain" Him to "abide with us."

"And it came to pass, as He sat at meat with them, He took bread, and blessed it, and brake, and gave to them. And their eyes were opened, and they knew Him."

This supper at Emmaus has been invoked as an authority for departure from primitive Christian practice on two opposed sides. In the first place, those who advocate Evening Communions assume that this supper at Emmaus was a repetition by Christ of the Institution of the Holy Eucharist in the upper chamber on the eve of His death. In the second place it is quoted triumphantly by Roman Catholics, on the same assumption, as evidence that Communion in one kind was of Christ's institution. Now, we have no right whatever to say that Christ on this occasion repeated the Eucharistic Sacrament. He sat down to the ordinary evening supper with the two disciples, and used the ordinary benediction of the bread that every Rabbi or master of a house employed. The two disciples had not been in the upper room at the Institution of the Eucharist. It is not likely they had heard about it from the Eleven. It was not the peculiarity of the benediction that struck them. No—He took the bread in His hands, raised it, and brake and blessed—and then they saw the wounds in the hands.

A change had come over Christ by His death and Resurrection. We know how that all great events, great sorrows, great joys do alter men; and those exceedingly great sorrows and agonies of Good Friday, and the marvellous Resurrection had wrought a mighty visible exterior change in Christ, so that the two, though they saw Him, did not recognize Him, yet their hearts burned within them; they were sure they had seen Him, heard the voice before, but could not be certain it was He Himself, till He took the unleavened wafer and raised it over the table and brake—and then they saw the nail prints in the hands—and at once, with a flash, perfect recognition came. They had invited Him to the ordinary meal, and He assumed the place of authority as the Maker and Giver of bread, as the Rabbi or teacher, and they saw that He was one with power and authority. He shewed Himself to be—not the guest, but the head of the family;

F

and whilst eating with them declared Himself as the Giver of all good things. These two may have been in the wilderness when He broke bread and miraculously fed a multitude, and He may have, in some way, recalled to their remembrance His action on that occasion, and this, joined to the sight of His pierced hands, convinced them Who He was; but most certainly they had not been in the upper chamber at the Institution of the Eucharist.

"And He vanished out of their sight. And they said one to another, Did not our heart burn within us, while He talked with us by the way, and while He opened to us the Scriptures?"

Christ had found the disciples sorrowing; He left them full of joy. And so has it been ever since. Into the midst of our griefs, in the time of desolation, in the hour of need, Christ comes to us, associates Himself with us, and then turns our heaviness into joy—that joy which, like His peace, passeth not away, and which no man can take from us.

"And they rose up the same hour, and returned to Jerusalem, and found the Eleven gathered together, and them that were with them, saying, The Lord is risen indeed, and hath appeared to Simon. And they told what things were done in the way, and how He was known of them in breaking of bread."

The two men act at once on what they know. We see in

this the energy and promptitude of their characters; not only so, but also they show us how, in Christ's religion, we are members one of another, and how we must communicate to others of what we have received. If one member suffer, all the members suffer with it; if one member be honoured, all the members rejoice with it—for we are all, though many members, one body in Christ Jesus.

NOTE: Captain Conder has suggested a new site as the Emmaus of the Gospel, at Khamasa, about three and a half miles S.E. of Atab and sixty furlongs from Jerusalem. I cannot see that the grounds are satisfactory for such an identification.

If Emmaus be properly Hammath, this implies the presence of hot springs; but if from Ammosa, or Mosa, with the article before it, it means the Pass, and applies well to Colonia, where is no warm spring. Josephus distinctly tells us that a colony of Roman veterans was settled at Emmaus, which thenceforth changed its name to Colonia, and there is Colonieh to this day.

It is true that Josephus says, "Now Emmaus, if it be interpreted, may be rendered 'a warm bath' useful for healing," but the Gemara (f. 45, 1) says, "Mosa is Colonieh. Why is it called Mosa? Because it passed free from tribute to the Emperor." The explanation is after rabbinic taste, and wrong. At Colonieh there is an abundant spring, but it is not warm, at all events now. Colonieh is not sixty stadia from Jerusalem, or between seven and eight miles, but considerably less. The road, however, is so mountainous and winding, that it may have been roughly called more than it really was. Moreover, the return of two disciples to Jerusalem, with the expectation of still finding the Apostles assembled, implies a shorter distance than a walk of over two hours.

Appendix.

ON THE SITE OF THE HOLY SEPULCHRE.

CAPTAIN CONDER has attempted an entirely new identification of the site of Calvary and of the Holy Sepulchre from that which is traditional, and this has been accepted by Dr. Cunningham Geikie in his "The Holy Land and the Bible," and by Sir Wm. Dawson in his "Egypt and Syria," as well as by others. Captain Conder takes a rounded hill, with two hollows in the precipitous face, which may in certain lights be taken to have a remote likeness to a skull, as the Calvary, or Golgotha, of the Gospel. This hill is situated outside the Damascus Gate of Jerusalem, on the North side, and is near the tomb of Jeremiah. Dr. Geikie quietly rejects the accepted site as being impossible, because it is within the walls of the city, whereas Calvary was without. Now, it is pretty evident that the accepted site was originally outside the walls; the still apparent traces of old Jewish tombs in the rock prove this, for the sepulchres were all anciently "without the gate."

Moreover, we know that Bezetha, the new town, was formed to the North and West, taking in within its circumference a large part of the suburbs, and the new wall including this was carried in a sweep from North to West by Agrippa I. after the death of our Lord, and this would take in the site of Calvary, which was before outside the Garden Gate. That tradition should retain the recollection of the true site of Calvary and the Holy Grave can hardly be doubted, as the Church remained at Jerusalem from our Lord's time ; moreover, a temple dedicated to Venus was erected by Hadrian on the site, to desecrate the spot sacred to Christians, just as a temple was erected with the same dedication at Bethlehem to desecrate the Cave of the Nativity. These temples at least stamped the spots as those which in the second century—that is, about A.D. 120, or less than a century after our Lord's Death, were venerated as the scenes of his Birth and Death.

Eusebius, born 264, mentions the excavations made on the traditional site of Calvary. It is almost inconceivable that the early Church should not have remembered the true site of the Death and Resurrection, and should have completely ignored that which Captain Conder is pleased to suggest, and which has little to recommend it except a fanciful resemblance to a skull, only to be discovered in a certain light, and only to be traced by a lively imagination.

THE END.